I Have a Story to Tell

© CAMFED International 2004

Photographs © Mark Read and CAMFED International 2004

Design © Saskia Janssen
Printed & bound by The Good News Press Ltd

First published in Great Britain in 2004 by

CAMFED International
22 Millers Yard
Mill Lane
Cambridge
CB2 1RQ
UK
www.camfed.org

ISBN 0-9532907-1-9

1st edition

I Have a Story to Tell

Celebrating 10 years of CAMFED International

Photographs by Mark Read

Acknowledgements

We want to thank the many organisations and individuals who have given so much to CAMFED's work over the past ten years. This book stands as a tribute to your commitment and generosity.

We also want to give special mention to those individuals without whose financial support and creativity this book would still be an idea – Mary Mount, Charles Cotton, Fiona Eberts, Theo Sowa, Maud Blair, Mark Read, Saskia Janssen and John Hamilton.

Foreword

I am proud to introduce you to a story of hope for Africa. This book celebrates the achievements of some wonderful young women, whose dignity and strength shine through their every word and photograph.

Each of these young women has turned her experience of poverty into a source of strength and compassion. Each has made remarkable changes in her own life and in the lives of her family and community. They are now working together to ensure that other children and young people secure futures worth having. These are extraordinary young women – and yet we know that there are millions of other young African women who could and would do the same if they had access to education.

The common thread through all their lives is the power of education. If their stories teach us anything, it is that the struggle for education for all must be won, and that when it is, other struggles – against poverty, war, ignorance and disease – will become easier to win.

In solidarity,

Graça Machel

Come is the day when our voices can be heard from the top, producing an echo that awakens all those who are asleep.

Introduction

On the day this book was published, it was estimated that 24 million girls in Africa were unable to attend school. Without support from CAMFED, the young women who tell their stories in this book would have been among them.

Education costs money. Most schools in Africa charge families a small fee to cover their overheads. Added to this is the cost to families of ensuring their children have decent clothes to wear to school, and basic essentials such as pens and paper to enable them to learn. Yet for many parents, these costs are beyond their means for all their children. The result is that they are often forced to make the agonising choice as to which of their children should attend school. It will usually be the boy of the family; he is seen as more likely to gain employment on leaving school, a vital consideration for parents who have no other security in old age.

When a girl is excluded from education, she faces a harsh and frightening future. She has few safe employment opportunities and with little confidence to draw on, her choices in life become extremely limited. She cannot negotiate in relationships and as a young woman, she is one of the group most vulnerable to AIDS. She is condemned to a vicious circle of poverty and exclusion, an inheritance that she will pass on to her children.

This is where the story of CAMFED begins. Our first priority is to get girls back into school by tackling the root cause of girls' exclusion – poverty. We work with village chiefs and local teachers to find the children who are out of school and offer their parents the opportunity for their daughters to attend, an offer that not one family has refused in our more than ten years' experience. We support girls from the same communities so that they can go to school in groups and assist each other once they are there, ensuring that no girl is left feeling isolated or bewildered. We work with schools to create an environment in which all children can give of their best, and can take the next steps in their lives with confidence and ambition.

Thousands of young women have completed their education with our support, among them doctors, lawyers, teachers and businesswomen. Their combined initiative led to the creation of CAMA, the CAMFED Association, which is uniting young women across Africa and calling for all girls to be given their right to education. These young women are now leading CAMFED's work to reach other girls in their communities and ensure that they too have the chance to go to school. Together, we are multiplying the number of girls who benefit. We began by supporting a group of thirty-two girls in rural Zimbabwe; ten years on, we are supporting 150,000 in Zambia, Ghana, as well as Zimbabwe.

Girls' education delivers far-reaching benefits for us all. It leads to improved health and brings economic growth. It is heralded as the most effective weapon we have in the global fight against AIDS. It means women can negotiate in relationships and choose how many children to have, and in turn ensure those children go to school – a virtuous cycle.

This book gives voice to young women whose stories tell of the extraordinary potential that is unlocked when girls receive an education. Yet their stories should not have to be extraordinary. They are a wake-up call, showing us all what a different place the world could be if all girls went to school.

Lucy Lake, Director of Programmes, CAMFED International

When I heard that I was to go to school, the force of gravity was really jealous, because I could have jumped and touched the clouds!

...

Barbara Bongo, speaking in 1995, now a secondary school teacher in Zimbabwe.

Fiona Muchembere

We are young women who have defied the odds and are going to achieve even more.

In the journey of my life I've encountered many hurdles that have left me stronger. They were actually steps up the ladder. I have managed to be where I am now mainly because of my education. To me education is a weapon against poverty.

I grew up in a society where it is said that the only course a woman would pass is marriage. I come from a family where there is no one qualified for any professional job, where there is no one who has been to university. I am actually their pioneer. And in a community where there is no lawyer, I have introduced diversity. Parents, not only mine, have come to appreciate that it is important to educate a girl-child.

In my practice there are fifteen lawyers, thirteen of them are men. There is no difference – we are all qualified by the same degree. My clients are mainly banks and companies and usually these sectors are highly patriarchal. I prove to them that I can advise and guide them and they respect me and my ideas.

The legal profession is now more gender sensitive. In the Supreme Court, there are three female judges out of a bench of seven. You find that lawyers prefer to appear before a female judge because they listen, they get down to the facts of the matter, they have more patience.

I would like to become an advocate for law reform. There are still areas in which I feel the law is repressive to women. The Births and Deaths Registry, for example, does not allow a woman to get a certificate for her own child. In law, she is allowed. In practice, she cannot. The registrars will say, 'Go and get your husband or a letter from him.' I want to work for a situation in which everyone is able to claim their right through the law.

My grandmother laid the foundation for me. She gave me the picture of a good mother. When I was in Form One, I told her, 'I don't like maths. It's very difficult.' She told me, 'You don't say that. You say you are going to excel.' And I did.

...

*Fiona Muchembere, **now a qualified lawyer in Zimbabwe.***

Lucia Punungwe

When education was introduced in Zimbabwe, mostly it was boys who were sent to school and not girls. The parents were so poor they could not afford to send both. It was believed that educating boys was an investment because a man would marry, bring his wife home and continue to support his parents. But my parents struggled to send us all, boys and girls, to school.

My father and mother depended on subsistence farming. We grew crops mainly for our own consumption and sold very little. I still remember my father setting off with a big sack of groundnuts on his shoulders to walk kilometres and kilometres selling them from one village to the other. I remember seeing him coming back very tired and hungry as well as dirty with the dust from the road.

When I finished primary school, I could see many people filled with joy saying that they were proceeding to secondary school. I just broke into tears. I had passed very well and was even the second highest in the school but I could not proceed with my education – my father had no money because of the drought that same year.

I will never forget the help that CAMFED rendered me for my education. I felt accepted and loved. I worked hard in school. I even became the head girl. I got to solve other people's problems since every girl consulted me when in trouble. In the final exams, I reaped what I had sown and achieved six As and three Bs.

Education removed a blanket of darkness from my face such that I can now see very well. I am able to communicate with you because I learnt English at school. I can even teach others. Had it not been for my education, I would probably already have many children to care for.

In Zimbabwe there are many girls like me who cannot afford to go to school. The dream has come true for some of us and we are helping others to achieve their dreams.

...

Lucia Punungwe coordinates CAMFED's support to give thousands more girls in Zimbabwe the opportunity of education.

Siphelani Chomuzinda

My toughest time was when I became a widow. It was 1998 and I was eighteen. My husband left me with a two-week-old baby.

My husband was in the military. He was taken to the military hospital. They released him the very same day and he came back home alone. The following day he passed away. The military provided me with transport to bring his body to our home area of Murewa.

To lose the one you love most is not easy. I used to cry. People looked down on me – I was now just a single parent. My mother was not working. My father was not working.

With a grant from CAMFED, I started my own business raising poultry. The first year was full of ups and downs. After keeping two batches I realised that most people in my area didn't have money to afford chicken. I moved my business to town. This I found tough but through my determination and commitment and great inspiration from other women, my business has been made easier. I can say that my living standard has changed. I am now able to look after my child and myself.

I am growing up in mind and in business. Now I have touched the stars and I am not going to give up till I reach the moon.

...

Siphelani Chomuzinda advises and supports other young women in her community who are starting their own businesses.

Spiwe Rare

When I was seven years old, my father took another wife. My stepmother beat me and bought her own child a uniform and a good pair of shoes, but not me. I used to go to school with my torn clothes. In the afternoon I would make cardboard slippers and wear them on my way back home as it was too hot to step on the soil in the heat.

My classmates laughed at me, but I did not lose hope because I wanted to do my best and be an example to my family as I was the first girl to be sent to school in the whole family.

After I finished school, I started my business with a grant from CAMFED to buy seven metres of school uniform cloth and three metres of check-check for collars, sleeves and yokes. I managed to make six uniforms for girls and sell them in the community. After that, people came to me with their orders for more uniforms both for girls and boys. I used my profits to help my family members, and help children in the community by giving them pens and exercise books for their schooling.

Now it makes me very happy because my business is going well and I have enough income to help my brothers and sisters to go to secondary school. I have also built my own house which is a marvel to my community.

...

Spiwe Rare is the first woman in her community to build her own house made of bricks.

I was really desperate for education. I was the only source of hope in my family since my brothers did not succeed at school and I am the only girl and the last born. I was trapped in the cycle of poverty, and you know poverty sticks like glue. But I was ready to take up that challenge of breaking the cycle of poverty in my family through my education!

...

Chipo Maravanyika is now a community health worker and the breadwinner for her family, supporting her parents and three elder brothers.

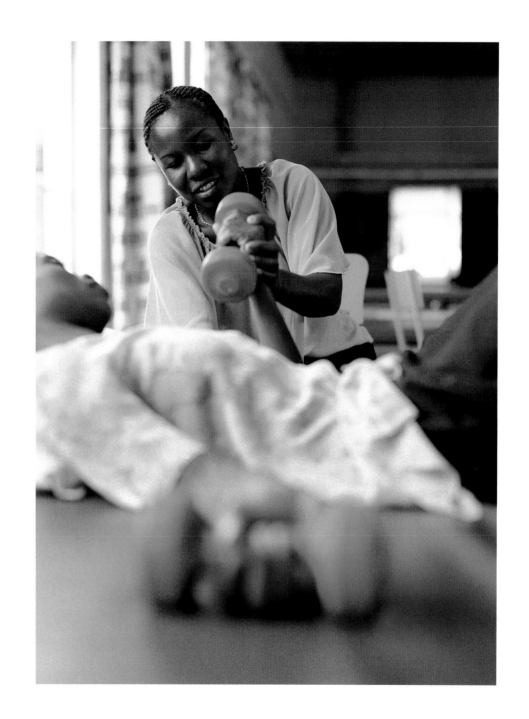

Primrose Mandishona

People say of me, 'If that was what she was and this is what she is, then maybe we too have the chance to do something different.'

I was around nine months old that day. My mother and grandmother went to the fields. They left me and my sister in the hut where people stay to scare the baboons. My mother came back to find the hut on fire. My sister had pulled me out from the hut but the burning thatch was falling on me.

I was taken to the hospital, and for many years I was receiving treatment. I developed contractures, which affected my posture. I was transferred to Gweru for a graft but it failed. It is by God's grace that I am not a psychiatric patient.

I can't recall the pain, but now because of the pain I see in other children, I know it was painful. I now understand the severity of my burns. I had known the practicalities. I had the experience and now I understand the theory. Today, it's great because I understand the problems and work with them. Especially when I am treating children with burns, placing them in the saline baths, I will say, 'You don't have to cry. We want you to be well. I was also burnt when I was very young.' And I will show them my scars and they are happier. It becomes much easier for them and for us to treat them.

It has been a long journey to become a physiotherapist. I applied in 2000 and got a 'regret'. I applied again only to receive another 'regret'. The Principal, Mr Tarasana, wrote to me giving advice. I applied again and got an interview. I told them, 'No matter how many times you regret me, I will not give up.' I got my place. I knew it was the job for me.

I want people to feel secure. I help people who are disabled believe they have a place in society just like everybody else.

...

Primrose Mandishona is training as a physiotherapist.

Wanzirayi Meke

In 1993, when my father lost his job at the mine where he worked, that was when the lot fell heavily on my family. It was then that my family had to move to the rural areas. I was in Form One and my father insisted that he had no money to pay for those of us who were in secondary to continue in school.

My sister and I decided we needed to get employment to help the family but with only my primary school completion, I had no choice of a job. So I was employed as a maid.

I was not used to being given a list of things to do but I was soon going to learn. I worked for a lady and in the morning as she left for work she would give me the schedule for the day. I did all the work and sometimes the task was beyond one person. I used to do all the household duties and to feed the children and as if that was not enough, she would come home in the evenings and yell at me. That was the hell I was in. It is very hard to work for a person who does not appreciate you. I tried by all means to please my employer, but she never appreciated it.

That is when I realised the importance of education. I realised that if one is educated one can do better things. I used to see people my age going to school but I could not join them.

Though the money that I earned was little, I helped my family. I worked for one year and one month and early in 1996, I was able to go back to school with the money I had saved. When people saw me going to school, they thought it was the joke of the year. I did not blame them because most people believe that if one is pushed out of school for such a long time it will be impossible to complete. I managed to prove them wrong.

...

Wanzirayi Meke enrolled in 2003 at the University of Zimbabwe to study business administration.

Angeline Mugwendere

When people say it cannot be done, they only mean it has never been done before.

I was born in Sadza – a rural district in Zimbabwe – a fact that was going to militate against my educational opportunities. My parents were subsistence farmers with little or no surplus to sell for basics, let alone school fees. I had no older brother or sister to look up to for support but four junior brothers and sisters.

During my first years at primary school no fees were required – just any dress, some food and a little encouragement. Life took a bitter turn when the government introduced fees. Uniforms were made compulsory and to add salt to the wound, the Economic Structural Adjustment Programme was put in place. I remember my parents getting so frustrated when in the same year the rains did not come. Rains were our source of livelihood.

I would hear people in the community say things like 'manhanga anowira kune vasina hari' (those who harvest so many pumpkins are often the people who do not have clay pots to cook them in). I was so very hurt to hear such things. What they meant was that here I was, an intelligent child and bright in class, but that my mother couldn't capitalise on this because she could not afford to pay for my education.

I vividly recall wearing a torn dress to school, no vaseline to hide my cracked skin, no shoes and little to eat. I felt so vulnerable and uncomfortable. I was sent home to collect fees which I knew and understood too well were not there to be collected. We had to skip two or three meals just to keep going. →

→ I remember the times when I just could not stand the teasing by the well-off students and I withdrew from drama and debating.

Back at home I had a lot of duties as the eldest child. I had to fetch firewood and water, help in ploughing, and assist my mother to sell vegetables. Sometimes I used to go and work in other people's fields. My mother would say, 'No, no, no, you don't need to go with me,' but I realised that if my family was to survive, I had to join her. Even if my pen got finished I wouldn't go and tell my mother because I wouldn't want her to start worrying. It made me very innovative because at break-time, I would go to a teacher's house and say 'Can I wash your plates?' and in return they would sometimes give me a pen.

I scored the best possible results in my final year at primary school. I was not just the best at my school, but in the province, and one of the best in the country. And yet this success made me cry not for joy but out of pain. It made me realise the power of poverty against me getting into secondary school. More fees were needed than the primary fees my parents had struggled and scratched to get. It was then that CAMFED came in and committed to support me through my education, an education that has had an irreversible impact on my life.

I have ceased to be the Angeline my primary schoolmates used to know. I have acted on the potential that poverty had suppressed in me. I've made meaningful decisions not just for myself but to support my family and friends. I've learnt to challenge oppressive situations and voice my objections whenever I realise someone's ignorance is being exploited. I have gained the confidence to be the real me.

...

Angeline Mugwendere, *leader of CAMA, the two-thousand-strong and growing network of young women in Zimbabwe who are uniting to develop their communities.*

Spiwe Matimba

I have a strong foundation for my life through education. I can say that education is my mother who managed to give me special love so I could stand up.

Some of my friends got involved in different things. Some decided to go in the streets and do robbery. Some decided to have early marriages and are now being ill-treated by their husbands. Some are prostitutes. And many of them have died due to AIDS.

Without my education, I just cannot imagine what kind of life I could be leading. I was one of the poorest girls to start off in my community and people treated me just like that. No one thought that my life would ever be transformed because to them it was all so very hopeless. Poverty had silenced me and I never thought I could rise from that curse. I absolutely agreed with my neighbours and just thought I was born in poverty and would die poor. After all, what else was there to believe?

With CAMFED's support, I started my own business. I am helping to pay school fees for my brothers and sisters. It really became my salvation when my baby got sick. When my child was always in and out of hospital, my business helped me meet all the hospital expenses and transport. My boyfriend who was the father of the baby had denied responsibility for the pregnancy for reasons best known to him and never lifted a finger.

At my child's death in 2000, I bought his coffin and bought food for all the people who came to mourn him. The community now view me with different eyes and, in a way, I am sure they envy this little girl and mother who could afford to take care of her own baby, even after death. A lot of other people are getting buried without a coffin, but I managed to let my baby go with some respect.

My business is a good way to earn a living and I am so proud of it. More girls should make the effort to start their own businesses not because they are single mothers, but because there is a lot of good in having an independent income in a marriage and within a family. You are respected and have got status. You are not considered a nonentity to be trampled on. Which is worth living for!

...

Spiwe Matimba, pictured with her new family, is now a community health worker and business mentor to other young women.

Faith Muzengi

I know from personal experience that parents really love to have their daughters in school and would do everything they could to ensure they remain there and succeed, but lack of funds thwarts their effort – education has become so expensive and beyond their pockets. But faced with a situation where they have to choose between sending a daughter to school or starving the whole family, they just do not have any way out of such a cruel decision.

My own mother made a lot of sacrifices just to make sure I stayed in school.

One time my mother had to give me her only petticoat to wear under my beige uniform at secondary school. She gave it to me leaving herself with none. She said this as she handed it to me, 'Faith, my daughter, you are the one who is going to school and you deserve the best this house can offer you. You do the best and I know when you finish school and get employed you will always be able to buy me more petticoats.'

Another time she had to sell a bucket of maize at a third of the normal price and carry it on her head to the person who had bought it five kilometres away, just to have some money for me.

I know that poor parents might be poor when it comes to material things, but they have such a rich passion for education.

...

Faith Muzengi, pictured with her mother, trains young women across Zimbabwe in community health.

Winnie Farao

I know what it means to be once in poverty and now a figure of success.

My dad was a cook for a commercial farmer. My mother used to work in his fields. Our house was just within the fence of the farmer. With my brothers and sisters, I used to play with his children – Richard and Adam. I am sure they are now big men.

It was really a beautiful time for us because the farmer would ask my dad to cook extra food for us. We used to go fishing. We used to ride horseback.

But the friendship was not equal. We always went behind them. When they said: 'Winnie, stop that now!' I would stop immediately. There was no way I could not comply. They could call me when I was doing my homework and I would have to go. My mum could not say no. My dad could not say no. It's something I think of now, but then it was the order of the day.

The farmer used to shout at my dad. These were my worst moments. To me it was very rude because my dad was old enough to be respected and I could not understand. My dad would rarely share with us those tough moments for him.

I always look at the positive side. The fact that I could have the opportunity of talking to them gave me confidence in speaking English. My mother was illiterate. She used to call me 'Miss English'.

But as someone told me, 'Winnie, your educational life has got scars. This is something to be proud of. You have something to say to your children, something to tell them.'

I have a strong zeal to help other girls to go to school. I understand the joy that was brought to my family and this I want to do for other girls and their families. I know that the energy that I and my colleagues give out is so life-giving. I will work flat out to see our intentions through. →

Winnie Farao has just graduated from the University of Zimbabwe with a first class degree in Psychology.

Yvonne Kapenzi

I now know who I am and what I want from life.

When I was only five years old, I went to stay with my uncle's family where I used to eat sadza and vegetables from the same plate with his seven greedy children. They were fifteen and above years. This was very hard, especially because the sadza would get finished when I had only eaten one mouthful. If I asked for more food, Grandmother would shout at me. At the age of six, some children were already attending their primary school but as for me, it was a different story. I was staying at home as a baby-minder, housemaid and cattle-herder.

I was released from that jail when my stepfather died. That is when my mother returned with my three stepbrothers, and I went to school. People in the community used to give us second-hand clothes and we used to go to school barefooted, slipping over small stones when we were rushing for lessons. Sometimes I would admire those businessmen's children who used to have expensive school shoes and socks, packed lunch with delicious food, and satchels on their backs. This gave me the inspiration to do my best at school.

My teacher used to like me very well because I was bright in class. But I still remember the children from the well-off families. They used to put a line on the desk to demarcate where we, the poor children, had to sit. If we crossed the line they would beat us with a ruler. At home, we lived in one hut which served as the bedroom, the granary, and the kitchen. It meant that our clothes always smelled of smoke from the cooking fire and sometimes children ran away from me at school because they said, 'You smell of smoke all the time.'

→

→ Life became very hard for me when I completed my primary education. My mother was saying, 'Ah, you are so bright but I don't know where I can get the money to send you to secondary school.' She tried to talk to my uncle, but he said, 'It is better to send her brother. He is a boy and he can be responsible when he grows up.' While others went to secondary school, I stayed at home helping my mother weed in the fields, until a door opened unexpectedly. My former headteacher came and found us in the fields where we were weeding. He talked to my mother and I didn't know what they were saying. Then my mother called me and said, 'You are going to school.' I didn't believe the news. I just sat there and stared.

Before I received my secondary education, I feared that life would bind me and make me a slave. My hope was rekindled by my education; it transformed me into viewing life from a different perspective. It taught me to be myself and to have power over my life.

After leaving school I started my business of buying and selling spring onions. Now I am able to sell a variety of products. I am supporting my brothers through school. I am able to buy my own clothes. I have even built a hut so that we now have a bedroom separate from our kitchen.

...

Yvonne Kapenzi runs a successful business and is the first young woman in her community ever to secure a loan from a commercial bank.

Prisca Kanhukamwe

I never thought that one day I would look back and say, 'Gone are the days I was poor and never had any hope for the future.'

Born in a family of three children and staying at home with both my parents, life was tough but bearable until 1993 when my father got sick. By then I was in Form One and my mother had to find the means of getting medication for my father and paying for our school fees. She would go to the Binga fishing camps and sell fish in Bulawayo and Lupane. There were times when we could not pay the fees and I had to stay at home. There was nothing we could do and my father's health got worse, and so it was a matter of living every day and accepting the way that it was.

Life continued like this for three years, and then while I was writing my exams, my father was hospitalised. When I got my results, I had passed five, but it meant nothing because the day before my father had died. I knew that one day he was going to die, but I still could not take it.

I have never before had the courage to say that my dad died of AIDS, to admit that the disease is in my family.

But thankfully, despite it all, I had my education, and now I have had time to grow up and know what I want in the future. I am looking after my mother. I think she has suffered a lot and now it is high time I take all the responsibilities. I am making sure that my young brother completes school.

...

Prisca Kanhukamwe **is a businesswoman in Bulawayo.**

In my work I meet many young people whose lives have been crushed by AIDS. Sharai had been left forever by her mother with a disabled brother. Her mother was married but due to some family affairs, the father divorced her as well as his children. The mother wanted to take care of her children and so she started selling at a certain market place to make money. Because of the high cost of living she could not meet all the family expenses with the little she earned from the market. She then became a commercial sex worker. She only did that for a few years before she started suffering from AIDS. Sharai dropped out

of school to care for her sickly mother. Unfortunately, her mother died and Sharai remained with the burden of her disabled brother aged nine, alone. Her mother spent a week in the mortuary since no relative had come to organise the funeral. The church volunteered to bury her. A number of teachers gave the family maize, soap, cooking oil and salt for the two children to survive on. Sharai has lost a number of things in life – her mother as well as so much of her schooling. Only this heavy burden was left for this girl. It is a burden that we now help her to shoulder.

Mary Nyagura works with local authorities in Nyanga to identify and support children left vulnerable by AIDS.

AIDS, AIDS, what do you want?
You kill people
You have taken my father and now my mother
What shall I do in the world without parents?
I don't have food to eat
I don't have clothes to wear
AIDS, AIDS, what do you want?
You are finishing us all.

...
*Child reciting the poem she
wrote for her class, taught by
Cynthia Chinhamo.*

Angeline Mugwendere

A number of my friends went on to sleep with 'sugar daddies' in return for cash to remain in school. Many of them were orphaned and living with aged and poor grandparents after their parents died of AIDS. Others were living alone as their parents were working far away on commercial farms or in mines.

It might sound a foolish decision they took but I knew it was not foolishness that forced them to do that. It was the effect of exclusion. They wanted an education and to be recognised because of it – to be looked up to by their communities. They wanted their families to be proud of them when they got a degree or when they came back to work in local clinics as nurses. I admired the nurses and teachers so much myself, but at least I had the hope of becoming one of them because someone was paying my fees. For these other girls who were my friends, it was just so out of reach.

I do not blame them for getting desperate, for none of us wants to be excluded. We all want to outlive those who came before us and to make a greater contribution than they did. They took the shortest possible route to be included in the system, dangerous as it was. These girls were not acting out of stupidity but because they were stuck in a vicious circle of poverty.

If only they had been as lucky as I was, they would be alive today. If only they had got into school and remained, they would not have become so desperate. My friends would have turned the sugar daddies down as I did. But how could they have done this, excluded from school as they were? They could not even listen to my words, as to them it sounded like mockery. They would look at me and say, 'If only you knew what it means to be out of school, with a head so full of ideas, but to have people look at you as foolish because you did not get educated.'

The courage and self-esteem I and my colleagues in CAMA gained in our years through school have given us the confidence to turn these men down and not to lean on them for financial support.

The bottom line is that it would be so much easier for girls to protect themselves if they just had the opportunity to go to school.

...

Angeline Mugwendere is the director of CAMA.

I am proud to be myself

My education gave me power over my life. There was no time when I needed this more than during the events that took place in April 2002. My boyfriend forced me to have sex without my consent. When this was discovered at my church, the elders took the two of us and said that we should now stay together as man and wife. To make matters worse, my mother even went on to say she would no longer stay with me as she suspected I was pregnant. I felt so unwanted. I talked to a woman in the community who later explained to my mother about the consequences I would face if I stayed with such a guy.

Not to marry him was the best decision I made in my life because otherwise I would not have managed to be the person I am today. I am glad that all the people who were trying to force me to get married now know that I have a better role to play in the community. Forced marriage can affect a girl a lot; maybe she will be very young, she won't be prepared, and she won't be able to achieve her goals. If a man has paid lobola (brideprice) for his wife, then the family expects that wife to have a lot of children. They don't think about how she is going to support those children.

I have a role to play in helping children who face the same problems. When I move around the district, I hear people saying, 'Oh you are the girl who talks to the school children'. They praise me and I feel so happy about that. I am gaining community respect, and I am proud to be myself.

...

The writer wants her story told and has chosen to remain anonymous. She is now a mentor to vulnerable children.

Cynthia Chinhamo

When I have a son, I will tell him not to treat his children as we were treated. I will discourage him from being a polygamist. There is too much jealousy and the wives are not free. His children will starve as we did. There is competition between wives. If one is pregnant and they buy a nice maternity dress the other decides to get pregnant as well.

I used to question my dad's paternity because of the way he treated us. Even when I started to work for myself, Dad started trying to force me to take care of the rest of the family, which was too much for me. I would wish that other children's fathers were my own. I wished that we could vote for our fathers and I would not vote for him. I hope my son will only have one wife and fewer children so he can take care of them.

I will also tell my child that if you have your own money everything can be different. It's not fun being a poor daughter-in-law. You do all the work, carry out all the chores, but they will still disregard you. If you do not have your own cash, they want you to worship them. A poor person's voice is scorned, those with cash are given a chance to speak and are listened to.

Through my education, I have turned out to be totally different to what I thought I would become. I am now confident, independent and determined. My community now takes me as a leader. They have chosen me to be a pre-school teacher, a job that I love.

Children are so eager to learn. When you teach them a game or a rhyme they have good memories. They will pass on the message. If you teach them to pray before eating they will challenge you if you forget. By passing on what I teach them, they are helping to change things for the better.

...

Cynthia Chinhamo works as a pre-school teacher and health worker in her community.

Patricia Mangoma

I remember when my father gave me Z$20 as bus fare to go to an interview at Nyadiri Teachers' College. I used Z$9 to get to the college and whilst I was there the transport costs increased, and on the way back I was supposed to pay Z$16, so I had to borrow money from a friend. At home that placed pressure on my mother who had to help me find that money. We had to do piece work until finally I had enough to send back.

It was after that that I applied for a grant to start my own business. My proposal was successful and I worked hand in hand with my local headteacher who gave me books and other support. He encouraged me to work hard. My business became a family business as they really supported me. I used the first profits to expand my business. The rest I used to support my brothers and sisters at school and I also contributed groceries for the family. And when interviews came up for other posts, I was able to use my own money to attend.

I began involving other young people in my community by creating employment for them and at the same time training them so that they too could start their own businesses. With this I gained community respect, and I did not stop there. Since people in my community acknowledged me, my confidence was boosted and I then started working with the local schools, teaching the children about opportunities after school. Members of the community were using me as an adviser. Even my parents consulted me on family issues.

Today, when looking to the past, it seems like a dream, but that was the reality – and because of it, right now I can stand in front of people and encourage them so that they too can transform their lives.

...

Patricia Mangoma, pictured on the right, now coordinates a micro finance scheme to enable school-leavers around Zimbabwe to start their own businesses.

Rudo Gore

When I completed my primary education in 1989, I was looking forward to secondary school, but unfortunately my parents could not afford to pay my school fees. I asked them if they would allow me to go and work as a housemaid and they agreed. I worked for two years from 1990 to 1992. That was when I started to see what the world was and what it meant to me. I was being paid Z$20 a month. I spent Z$15 and kept Z$5. That Z$5 I was putting in a tin as my security. In 1992 I explained to my mother that I wanted to proceed with my education using the money I was keeping.

It's unfortunate that the secondary school was very far from home so there was a need to become a bush boarder, living in a hut I built for myself. My mother sold her only cow to help me. I still remember its name – Marooro. My mother said, 'Do you see that I have sold this cow for you, Rudo? When you go to school you should work very hard.'

During the rainy season, my hut, which we built with small poles of dagga and grass, fell down. We did not go to school that day while mending our hut with two other girls I was sharing it with. There was also the problem of not having decent clothes. I was going to school wearing the barmu-barmu skirt which my mother exchanged for ground nuts, and was also going to school walking barefoot. One of my classmates who came from a rich family gave me her sandals and the first day I started wearing them, the whole class clapped hands for me. I was very intelligent in class, but due to lack of decent clothes I was too shy to stand up and speak.

→

→ When I was in Form Four, my father passed away and this was during the drought. There was nothing to eat at home or to take to school. I and my young sisters and mother used to go and cultivate other people's fields so that we could be given maize to eat at home and to take to school. When the maize was finished, I spent a week and a half borrowing and eating other girls' food. At the end of the second week, I was really shy to eat others' mealie-meal. So I was waking up very early and if I saw others preparing porridge, I ran away or said, 'You can eat. I am satisfied.' At lunchtime I was remaining at school while others went to prepare lunch.

I thought of going home, and that is the time that CAMFED provided me with a uniform and porridge at school. I will never forget it.

After school I received training on cutting and designing, and I came back to my community to train other girls and young women. At first, the young women were not coming for the training, so then I had to go round to find out what the community wanted because some of the girls in Mola were not allowed to come and be trained, because their families thought that the girls would become prostitutes. But I continued to motivate the parents of the girls.

Now we have big meetings in the community and all the people come. The attitudes of the people in the community have really changed and they now want to be involved in all the activities. I have motivated the community to believe in girls' education and pay school fees for their children.

...

Rudo Gore leads a large and growing team of young women in Nyaminyami who are working to tackle poverty and develop their communities.

Because you are now an educated girl, remember that people will judge how educated girls behave when they look at you. Remember the old, the poor and the marginalized who are in your community. Don't forget that you can still carry wood and water. Look around you, see who needs your help and offer it.

*Part of the philosophy of CAMA,
the young women's network.*

Chief Mutekedza

*Girls without education
are like refugees in their
own Motherland.*

There had been fifteen years in my chiefdom with no chief until I was appointed. There was a lot of excitement and expectation from the people. I visited each family and collected information on family size, income and setbacks. My findings were shocking. Parents were dying and there were many child-headed households. There was evidence of great poverty. I have all this documented at my court.

I realised that people were living in these intolerable situations without knowing where to go for advice. They felt chiefs were too big to talk to. All wrong. In my community we can shake hands with one another. I have regular meetings with my community where we discuss issues of concern.

The security of girls is one of the main topics. Girls should not be afraid in their community. I do not tolerate any form of abuse and have caused seven men to go to jail for abusing girls. After realising the number of sensitive questions brought to my court and how shy most girls were to disclose information, especially of an intimate nature, I appointed a woman assessor to the chief's court. We must understand that many girls cannot repeat the trauma of what has happened, yet they are expected to say it again and again. Now, girls can share with other women and many cases are surfacing.

I have seen how the poor and disadvantaged are always trampled upon and exploited. An education gives people confidence and self-belief. Girls without education are like refugees in their own Motherland. They marry in darkness expecting their husbands to look after them, but when a husband loses his job he has nothing to offer and chases his wife away. Education is our prosperity. As chiefs, we are concerned about the well-being of our community and education is one way of safeguarding it.

The battle against poverty can never be won until all our girls are in school. I am working with my community to bring all our daughters to school.

...

Chief Mutekedza **is a senior traditional leader in Zimbabwe.**

Charity Masango

I was born after the war, on 18th July 1980. I was the first child in a family of six. My father was working as a tailor, and because he had only gone up to primary school, he could not secure a decent job. After just four years, my father lost his job and we had nowhere to live.

Provision of basics like food and clothing deteriorated to such an extent that we had to get all these from our church. We sometimes slept without eating anything and had sacks as blankets. Our house was a shanty house, concrete floor, no doors, no furniture. One day, the pupils in my class were taught about shantytowns and later on I was surprised to find our yard flooded with my schoolmates, laughing. They had come to look at our house as a good example of a shanty house. I was regarded as an outcast.

Only later, when I was doing my fieldwork as a district coordinator, did I realise that my experiences were like training to me. I have become so committed to helping other people in situations like mine. I have grown strong and now share my background with children in school.

I am currently involved in counselling abused children, since I was once a victim myself. My first aim is to have perpetrators behind bars, and with the support from the police, ten cases of abuse have recently been reported, investigations made and people arrested and remanded in custody. While some of them are out on bail, others are serving for the crimes they committed.

It is on everyone's lips now in Chikomba that children need a high level of protection from abusers. This is a fact that is constantly reinforced by Assistant Inspector Chikwababa. He assists us a lot and even goes beyond his job expectations. He is committed to helping children not only in the district but across the country.

I do promise that I will do my best to make Chikomba a better place for children to grow up in than it was for me.

Charity Masango, pictured with Assistant Inspector Chikwababa, works with police and other local authorities to help children in Chikomba.

Education has sown a seed in me, which is growing and flowering to produce other seeds, the seed of lifting the value of girls and women in the communities around me. I now understand that women can be recognised as important people in the community, and I can communicate freely bringing all my views and discussing them with people, even those in high positions.

Esther Jena is now a business administrator.

Lilian Munongowarwa

I am not ashamed of letting people know what I have been through. One of my close relatives forced himself on me and after a month I discovered I was pregnant. When I gave birth my parents took me back home. That was the most difficult time of my life. People would not believe me. They accused me of seducing him.

I stayed at home for less than a month before my mother became ill. She was admitted to hospital but she did not recover and finally she passed away. At her death I was left to take care of my baby and my father who had become mentally ill. At times my father got lost and at times lost his clothes, so I had to go in search of him. The situation worsened and he could not walk on his own, he had to use a wheelchair. He finally passed away.

Life without parents is not easy. I was alone and had no way to go out and look for work because there was no one to look after my baby while I was gone. My younger brother later joined me. We worked in the fields so hard to get something to thrive on. We grew and sold vegetables. I also started a broiler-keeping project. It was initially difficult, but the other girls whose business projects were up and running supported and advised me through it all.

My business was so successful that I expanded it. I started peanut-butter processing. From the profits I got I managed to buy clothes and food for myself, my brother and my child. I also began helping some other children in my community to remain in school by paying their fees.

→

→ I am now a community health adviser and I am trying to help the gold-panners. They are digging trenches to get gold – they have even dug under a railway line and it is very dangerous. When I first came here I was so touched by the way people are trying to make ends meet. They use the money to buy dry buns so that they have a meal for the day. I couldn't take it as real that people are depending on dry buns for their full diet on a daily basis. Even worse are their clothes – they move about almost naked. Grandmothers who might be over sixty years of age travel for a distance of eight kilometres selling buns so that they will get money to support their orphaned grandchildren.

Young children of eleven and twelve are quitting school to look for employment. These children also go to join the gold-panners. It is not only money which they get. The girls also get pregnant. Mostly the men responsible would say to each other, 'Just ditch the child with her baby.' Girls are also getting sexually transmitted diseases. One young girl was even at primary school. She used to sell fruit and vegetables to the panners. She was impregnated and gave birth to a baby. The gold-panner refused to accept responsibility. She went home but there was nothing and she was forced to return. Many like her end up risking their lives over and over again. Some as young as seventeen years have two children and are surviving from hand to mouth.

In my work I'm doing all I can to protect girls. I hope my story of what I have overcome will open doors for those who find themselves suddenly orphaned and have to take up responsibility for the whole family.

...

Lilian Munongowarwa counsels children left vulnerable by AIDS, and works with health and social services to secure support.

Bianca Chaka

When I was seven, Mum and Dad broke up. Mum left the house without anything, not even a teaspoon. We needed food, clothing and education but she was unemployed. This did not make her surrender, she stood firm and fought for our survival.

We lodged in a single room and I was now a single parent's child. I remember my mother told us the story of a certain woman she knew who was also a single parent with two daughters. Later on in life one became a teacher and the other a nurse, and in the end they looked after their mother.

My mother would tell me, 'My daughter, take education as something very important in your life.' I think it was because my mother was not educated. Her dad died and her two brothers remained in school but she and her sister had to leave. Even now, if you are to compare the life she lived with that of her brothers, they are totally different.

We worked so hard for our education, even though other children used to laugh at us for being poor. I remember one time when I was in primary school, our teacher told us to clean the classroom. During the sweeping, I removed my shoes and the shoes were very torn inside. When my classmates saw those shoes they said throw them away. That was my one and only pair of shoes. They threw them away but I saw where they threw them and went and got them back.

It was in 1999 when my source of inspiration, my pillar, my everything, died. Mum left me at the age of seventeen and by that time I was still fresh into the world. I knew nothing.

Now I am twenty-two and I feel the future holds more in store for me. Freedom and education have brought light into my life. I managed to use my privilege wisely and now I am in possession of an academic certificate. I am happy that I have gained all I need in my life – to choose when to be married, who to associate with, to speak out – to be me. I can now cater for myself and for my sister since I am the breadwinner. I am glad I now have power to decide what is good and bad for me.

In the future I will tell my daughter about my mother and tell her to be herself, to be confident with herself, and I will stand easy as her pillar and her advisor.

...

Bianca Chaka is a teacher at her local primary school.

Judith Kumire

When I look back and celebrate what I did, I still come face to face with many girls that are calling for help. Their voices echo from all over Africa, yearning for the opportunity to access education and obtain freedom.

In life, most of us walk long and winding journeys, during which some make mere dents and others make huge impressions. My journey made an impression that haunts me and keeps my life awake.

As a young college graduate, I was posted as head of my first school in the most remote area of Nyaminyami District. I felt lonely, lost and hopeless. I was exposed to a new and harsh environment that I had not grown up in. I did not know then that this was going to be a wake-up call for me to help girls in Africa access education.

There were not many girls attending lessons at Mola Secondary School, which was the only secondary school in a hundred-kilometre radius. I would meet a few shy girls in classrooms, grouped together to provide each other with support and protection from the male-dominated environment. Their participation was negligible, so much so that one could easily think they were absent.

For every six boys enrolled there was one girl, but the census statistics showed that there were more women in Mola than men. I could meet women and girls fetching water at the borehole, grinding maize meal at the mill, moulding bricks, weeding in the fields and gardens, but during elections they were busy voting men into power. It touched me so much that the very people who are the main producers, who ensure that families are well fed, and form the backbone of economy and agriculture, were being denied the opportunity to get an education. Some of them even lived next to the school, but never knew what was going on inside the walls of the classrooms.

→

→ I worked in this remote rural area for ten years; I developed a deep consciousness and respect for the poor. I have understood how poverty impacts on communities and individuals and that one does not choose to be poor. It is a situation no one among us would want to be in. I shared their shattered aspirations and dreams, dreams that were never realised because of poverty. The decisions taken by the poor are not out of choice because there is nothing to choose from.

Intrinsically, I believe educating a girl child builds bridges between African culture and the modern world we are living in today. It is only poverty that makes people hide behind the saying, 'Our culture does not allow girls to go to school.'

The presence of just a few girls in the school was an indication to me that there were many more girls out in the community who could be yearning to come, but were hindered by poverty. Knowing that gave me the confidence to reach out.

Change takes place slowly but when the results manifest themselves, they are great and long lasting. CAMFED has breathed life into many disadvantaged girls who were hopeless and lost, as it did for me ten years ago. I used to see girls failing but I had no resources and nothing to offer but encouragement. Now things have changed and after ten years of hard work and patience, many of those same girls have become community activists. And today, with the opportunities created by CAMFED, so much has changed and many more girls are now benefiting from the educational system in Mola.

What I say is, even if girls lose a thread along the way, do not despair. Count on them, because today these girls can celebrate with me the results of our dedication and our belief in the emancipation of women.

...

Judith Kumire is Director of CAMFED Zimbabwe, supporting tens of thousands of girls. Some of her former students are pictured here.

Message from CAMA

We have set out to prove to the world that we are resourceful individuals able to act on ideas and provide solutions grounded in the realities of the life we lived. We are along this road together.

When we left school we did not run away from our communities. We are sharing with them the benefits of our education. We are working tirelessly for those who never went to school – helping them to build their lives and their confidence. Many of us are providing our local communities with goods and services through the businesses we have set up. Some have gained places at university pursuing law, medicine, political administration and business studies. Yet others are employed as doctors, auditors, teachers and nurses.

We have acquired freedom in every sphere of life – economic freedom through professions and enterprise, and reproductive freedom in deciding when to marry, who to marry and when to have a child.

We are so proud that we have achieved all this. This is the message that we bring to you so that you may understand the potential in a rural girl who, when given a chance, can do wonders for her family and community. With all this evidence, who then can argue against her education?

Some of CAMA's leaders are pictured here with Chief Mutekedza.

I used to go to school barefooted, with my face full of hunger. If only I get the chance, I will do something great.

...

Runyararo Mashingaidze *wrote this statement in a letter to CAMFED in 1993. Runyararo is now a doctor working at Harare General Hospital.*